PARANORMAL HANDBOOKS

HANDBOOK TO

STONEHENGE,
THE BERMUDA TRIANGLE
AND OTHER MYSTERIOUS LOCATIONS

BY TYLER OMOTH

Raintree is an imprint of Capstone Global Library Limited, a company incorporated in England and Wales having its registered office at 264 Banbury Road, Oxford, OX2 7DY – Registered company number: 6695582

www.raintree.co.uk
myorders@raintree.co.uk

Edited by Nate LeBoutillier
Designed by Philippa Jenkins
Picture research by Svetlana Zhurkin
Production by Kathy McColley
Originated by Capstone Global Library Limited
Printed and bound in China

ISBN 978 1 4747 2407 4
20 19 18 17 16
10 9 8 7 6 5 4 3 2 1

British Library Cataloguing in Publication Data
A full catalogue record for this book is available from

Acknowledgements
We would like to thank the following for permission to reproduce photographs: Alamy: JTB Media Creation, 26, 29 (middle right); Bridgeman Images: Look and Learn/Private Collection/Building Stonehenge, Jackson, Peter (1922-2003), 8; Corbis: Robert Estall, 14; D.A.Cameron, 20, 29 (top middle); Dreamstime: Philcold, cover (top), back cover; HL Studios, 29 (map); iStockphoto: duckycards, 23, 29 (middle left); Newscom: Kyodo News, 27, Stock Connection Worldwide/Andre Jenny, 15, 29 (top left); Shutterstock: Dmitry Pichugin, 16, elementals, 1, 7, Eric Isselee, 21, Evgeny Gorodetsky, 19 (bottom), Gimas, 22, Jacek_Kadaj, 25, Jarno Gonzalez Zarraonandia, 24, 29 (bottom left), jaroslava V, cover (bottom), 6, Kevin & Beverly Photography, 19 (top), Kiev.Victor, 28, 29 (top right), Nicram Sabod, 17, Photovolcanica, 18, 29 (bottom right), sergeisimonov, 12, Vezzani Photography, 5, Volina, 11, Wollertz, 4; SuperStock: Science Photo Library, 29 (bottom middle); Wikimedia: U.S. Navy, 10

Design elements by Shutterstock.

CONTENTS

Shrouded in mystery

From steamy jungles to frozen glaciers and barren deserts, people love to explore the unknown. Usually, with discovery comes understanding. Some places, however, defy understanding. A desert in California has stones that wander across the sand on their own. Monuments stand that are so old, no one knows who built them, how or why. An area of the sea where planes and ships simply disappear baffles scientists and scares passengers.

Are these places a result of natural **phenomena** with scientific explanations that are yet to be discovered? Or are they destined to forever be part of the **paranormal**, shrouded in mystery that cannot be explained by logic?

Not all are brave enough to try to discover why these places defy explanation. In every corner of the world, there are mysterious locations. One thing is undeniable: These places fascinate us. These places are the world's most mysterious locations.

phenomena very unusual or remarkable events
paranormal something that has no scientific explanation

STONEHENGE

Each year approximately 1 million tourists visit Stonehenge.

On the green countryside just outside of Wiltshire, England, stands a formation of large rocks that looks impossibly old. How long have the rocks been there? Who put them there and why? These are the mysteries of the **prehistoric** monument known as Stonehenge.

prehistoric from a time before history was recorded

Stonehenge is an ancient **concentric** stone circle. Scientific dating methods suggest that the stone monument is roughly 5,000 years old. So how could prehistoric humans construct such a thing?

More than 160 stones make up Stonehenge. The largest are sandstones that weigh as much as 40 tonnes. These stones are local to the area. The smaller stones, called bluestones, may have come from nearly 320 kilometres (200 miles) away from the Stonehenge site. How were they moved? Some scientists believe the builders used large sledges to haul the stones. Others believe they may have moved the stones using rafts on rivers.

concentric multiple circles surrounding a central point
monolithic formed of a single block of stone
archaeologist person who studies human life and culture

Stonehenge on the screen

Fascination with Stonehenge has made it a popular choice as a film location. In *Doctor Who*, Stonehenge was featured in a 2010 episode. In the episode a prison called Pandorica lay beneath Stonehenge, and it contained the most fearsome prisoner in the universe.

Why was Stonehenge built? It is possible that the **monolithic** circles may have served as pens for livestock. However, the arrangement of the stones suggests to astronomers that they were meant to chart the stars or act as a giant calendar. The stones could mark the passing of time by the way the Sun, Moon and stars cast their light on them.

Archaeologists have also found human remains at the site. Some scientists believe that Stonehenge may have been an ancient burial site, a hospital or a place for important religious ceremonies. Because Stonehenge was built in a time before recorded history, we may never solve all of its mysteries.

THE BERMUDA TRIANGLE

On 5 December 1945, five US Navy bombers flew out of
Fort Lauderdale, Florida, USA, on a training mission.
The squadron leader reported trouble with compasses before
all radio contact was lost. The five planes disappeared.

A search-and-rescue mission never found any sign of
the planes. Some think it's possible that they may have been
victims of the Bermuda Triangle.

The Bermuda Triangle is an area covering 3.9 million square kilometres (1.5 million square miles) over the southern Atlantic Ocean. Miami, Florida, USA, and the islands of Bermuda and Puerto Rico mark its three points. This area is one of the most heavily travelled sections of water for cargo ships and cruise ships in the world.

For reasons no one knows, many planes and ships have flown into the Bermuda Triangle never to reappear. These vessels vanish completely, along with all crew and passengers. More than 1,000 lives have been lost in the Bermuda Triangle over the past century.

How does this happen? No one knows for sure. Some have blamed rogue tidal waves. Others suggest that aliens or giant sea monsters are to blame. Scientists continue to search for more likely answers.

methane colourless and odourless flammable gas found naturally

Far out!

Could there be a spot like the Bermuda Triangle in space? Approximately 200 kilometres (125 miles) above Earth, the South Atlantic Anomaly has so much radiation that satellites can't function when their orbit passes through it. NASA has even reported laptops crashing when space shuttles passed through it.

Navigation is important when travelling. Scientists believe that magnetic fields or **methane** pockets might make the vehicles' instruments malfunction. The "Hutchison Effect" theory suggests that an electronic fog surrounds vehicles in the triangle. This fog creates instrument malfunction and erratic movement.

The mystery of the Bermuda Triangle has fascinated many for decades. There have been books, board games and TV programmes centred around the topic.

In recent years fewer vessels have encountered problems in the Bermuda Triangle. There may be a logical reason why so many ships and planes once disappeared there. Many people still want answers for these events of the past.

FREAKY FACT

Famous explorer Christopher Columbus wrote in his journal about the Bermuda Triangle. In September of 1492, Columbus reported rough seas with no wind and the compass shifting on its own.

MAGNETIC HILL

Drivers in Moncton, New Brunswick, Canada, notice something weird on one particular hill. At the base of the hill, they have to use the accelerator or their cars roll backwards. This is Magnetic Hill, where cars roll uphill.

Since the 1930s, tourists have driven to Magnetic Hill to test it out for themselves. Year after year, decade after decade, the phenomenon has continued to amaze drivers.

In 2010 a Japanese scientist called Kokichi Sugihara made a video to demonstrate what happens at Magnetic Hill. The video shows wooden balls rolling up four different ramps. A change in camera angle shows that the ramps are actually going down instead of up.

The same is true of Magnetic Hill. **Optical illusions** caused by the surrounding countryside make it appear that the cars are driving downhill. In truth they are actually going uphill. So, when the car is put into neutral, it will roll backwards.

Judy Dougan, manager of Magnetic Hill for the city of Moncton, doesn't believe the truth will dampen the enthusiasm of tourists. "The secret's out, but you have to come and experience it," Dougan said. "It's a unique experience."

optical illusion something that deceives by presenting a false visual representation of reality

THE MOERAKI BOULDERS

There are a lot of things to find during a walk along the beach. Seashells and pretty pebbles are all fun discoveries. But those who walk along the beach in Moeraki, New Zealand, will find something more – much, much more.

Giant **spheres** of rock rest on the beach like the forgotten bowling balls of giants. What are they? How did they get there? Why are they so perfectly round?

Moeraki legend says that the boulders are gourds washed ashore from a great voyaging canoe, called *Araiteuru*, from hundreds of years ago. The story says that *Araiteuru* carried a number of chieftains, but the canoe was wrecked upon a reef. All of the chieftains survived except one, called Hipo. The largest rock in the reef is called Hipo after this chieftain. In stormy seas, waves still break against it with amazing force.

sphere round solid shape like a basketball or globe

Though they are perfectly round, no sculptor shaped these boulders. They are actually made from clumps of **sediment** and sand that formed into a ball and grew over a long period of time. Scientists say that it took these giant stones 4 million years to reach their current size. Each stone is 2 to 3 metres (6 to 10 feet) wide and weighs as much as 7 tonnes. Locals have given them many nicknames, such as "eel pots" and "giant gobstoppers".

Though some of the boulders have been taken as souvenirs, the site is now protected so that the remaining boulders will remain on the beach.

sediment bits of sand or clay carried by water or wind

Sneaky stones

In California's Death Valley National Park in the United States, stones move across the desert floor, leaving long trails behind them.

It appears that they are moving on their own. But the rocks are actually carried by thin sheets of ice moved by wind during the winter.

THE OVERTOUN BRIDGE

The Overtoun Bridge
was built in 1895.

In south-west Scotland near the town of Dumbarton sits a scenic stone bridge. It appears to be an ordinary old walkway across a stream. For dog owners, however, it is a place of horror. In the past 50 years, about 600 dogs have leapt from the same spot on the bridge — 50 of them to their deaths. Why would the dogs do that?

There are many theories about why the dogs make the leap. Some tell of a local man whose ghost haunts the bridge. They believe the dogs can sense the ghost and are frightened to the point of panic.

A more scientific approach has discovered a number of wild animals such as mice, squirrels and mink living in the undergrowth beneath the bridge. Perhaps the dogs smell the animals and jump over the edge to investigate.

The Overtoun Bridge spans a ravine with a 15-metre (50-foot) drop into a shallow stream. The dogs don't know there's a large drop, but hundreds have found out the hard way.

No one knows exactly why dogs throw themselves from the Overtoun Bridge. But most pet lovers in Dumbarton have learned to take their pups for a walk elsewhere.

FREAKY FACT

A dog's sense of smell is at least 1,000 times more sensitive than a human's. Breeds with the most sensitive noses are used for hunting, police work and search-and-rescue.

TAOS HUM

Taos, New Mexico

In a small town in New Mexico, USA, some residents hear something that makes them feel uncomfortable. These people can hear the Taos Hum. Faint and low, the Taos Hum is only heard by about two per cent of the resident population. Scientists have not been able to work out what makes the noise or why only a few can hear it.

Located next to dormant volcanoes, the area around Taos consists of rugged terrain with man-made caverns. Some think that the government is conducting secret experiments there, and that the experiments create the noise. Others believe that an alien ship caused the crater in a nearby mountain peak. Perhaps aliens now live underneath the ground.

As usual, scientists believe something natural is at work. Perhaps a small percentage of the residents of Taos have very acute hearing. That could explain how they hear sounds that others do not.

To this day no one knows the cause behind the Taos Hum. It's possible that science simply hasn't discovered the true cause of the phenomenon yet. For those who travel there to hear the strange sound, most are disappointed. But some – a very select few – can hear a true mystery.

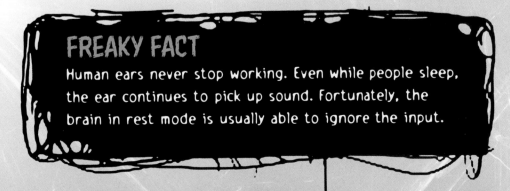

FREAKY FACT

Human ears never stop working. Even while people sleep, the ear continues to pick up sound. Fortunately, the brain in rest mode is usually able to ignore the input.

NAZCA LINES

For many years people saw nothing out of the ordinary in the Nazca Desert in southern Peru. But when humans discovered how to travel by air, they saw something from that vantage point that amazed and bewildered them.

Drawings of animals and at least one human on an enormous scale are visible in the desert. The **geoglyphs**, called the Nazca Lines, are the largest works of art in the world.

There are drawings of a bird several times the size of a football pitch, an enormous spider and even a man waving his hand. Hundreds of the figures are scattered throughout the Nazca Desert, created by a culture that no longer exists.

Archaeological discoveries show that the Nazcas dug shallow trenches that created the lines. No one knows how, or even if, they could ever see the end results of their own artwork.

Were the trenches calendars or some sort of paths? People have wondered if the Nazcas were trying to communicate with aliens. Modern scientists believe they may have used the drawings for ceremonial purposes. One thing's for certain: The Nazca Lines remain one of the world's greatest and most mysterious works of art.

geoglyph large picture or design created on the ground

A small island to the west of Japan is a diver's paradise. People travel from all over the world to Yonaguni to take in the unique beauty of the coral reefs and large populations of hammerhead sharks.

In 1986, one diver found more than he expected. Large stone formations on the seabed looked like the remains of buildings and monuments. Had the diver simply found amazing natural rock formations? Or had he found the remains of the lost city of Atlantis?

Some scientists believe these are natural rock formations created over thousands of years by currents and marine life. Not everyone agrees.

Markings on the stones suggest that the ruins are man-made. However, there are few clues to the culture that created them. The ruins are believed to be at least 5,000 years old. They include what appears to be a castle, an arch, five temples and a large stadium. Perhaps an earthquake or **tsunami** washed the mysterious city from the shore.

Man-made or natural, the Yonaguni Ruins allow divers to feel like they've entered a long-lost city underneath the waves of the ocean.

tsunami large wave caused by an underwater earthquake

HANDBOOK QUIZ

1. According to experts, why was Stonehenge built?

    a. to keep livestock
    b. to mark time
    c. for religious purposes
    d. all of the above

2. In which ocean does the Bermuda Triangle lie?

    a. Pacific
    b. Indian
    c. Arctic
    d. Atlantic

3. The largest Moeraki Boulder is named after which chieftain of Moeraki legend?

    a. Hipo
    b. Kokomo
    c. Jemaine
    d. Waititi

4. What type of animal tends to leap from the Overtoun Bridge?

    a. cats
    b. squirrels
    c. dogs
    d. frogs

5. In which country are the Yonaguni Ruins located?

    a. Uganda
    b. Japan
    c. Bolivia
    d. Cuba

Answers: 1-d. 2-d. 3-a. 4-c. 5-b.

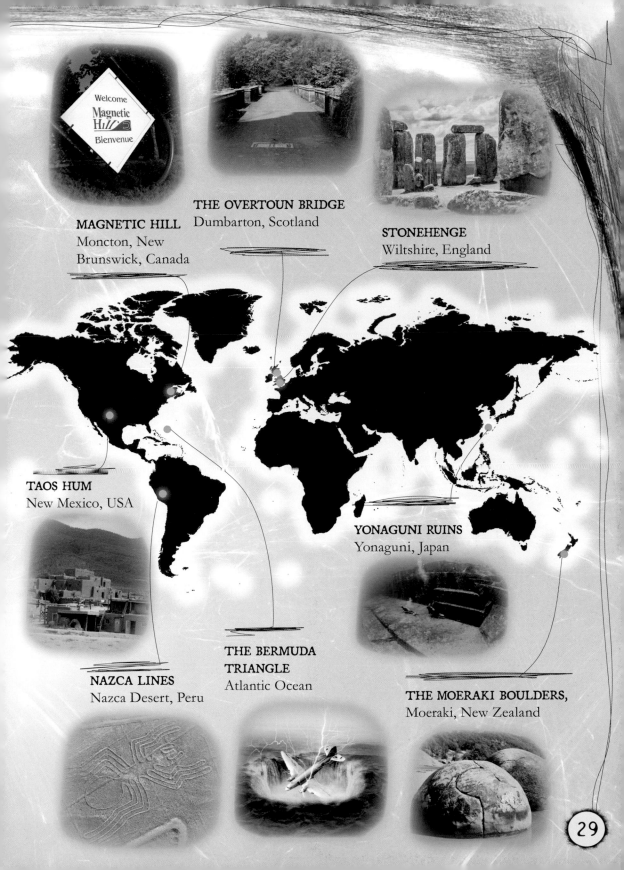

MAGNETIC HILL
Moncton, New
Brunswick, Canada

THE OVERTOUN BRIDGE
Dumbarton, Scotland

STONEHENGE
Wiltshire, England

TAOS HUM
New Mexico, USA

YONAGUNI RUINS
Yonaguni, Japan

NAZCA LINES
Nazca Desert, Peru

**THE BERMUDA
TRIANGLE**
Atlantic Ocean

THE MOERAKI BOULDERS,
Moeraki, New Zealand

29

GLOSSARY

archaeologist person who studies past human life and culture

concentric multiple circles surrounding a central point

geoglyph large picture or design created on the ground

methane colourless and odourless flammable gas found naturally

monolithic formed of a single block of stone

optical illusion something that deceives by presenting a false visual representation of reality

paranormal something that has no scientific explanation

phenomena very unusual or remarkable events

prehistoric from a time before history was recorded

sediment bits of sand or clay carried by water or wind

sphere round solid shape like a basketball or globe

tsunami large wave caused by an underwater earthquake

READ MORE

Non-fiction

The Bermuda Triangle (Solving Mysteries with Science),
Jane Bingham (Raintree, 2013)

Lost Cities (Treasure Hunters), Nicola Barber (Raintree, 2013)

Unsolved Archaeological Mysteries (Unsolved Mystery Files), Michael Capek (Raintree, 2015)

Fiction

Scooby-Doo: The Curse of Atlantis (You Choose Stories), Laurie
S Sutton (Curious Fox, 2015)

Soul Shadows, Alex Woolf (Curious Fox, 2013)

Tales of Mystery and Imagination (Usborne Classics Retold),
Tony Allan (Usborne Publishing, 2007)

INDEX